Stephen

Day of the Flying Leaves

www.willesdenherald.com

Independently published worldwide
via Amazon KDP 2021

'Annie' was first published in *Gargoyle*
'In the Waiting Room of the Western Eye Hospital' was first published
in *Southernmost Point Guest House.*
'Ballad' was first published in *Last Night's Dream Corrected.*
'Wake Up Call' was first published in *The Stare's Nest.*
'Winter Thoughts' was first published in *Stachtes English Wednesdays.*
Some of the poems previously appeared in Stephen Moran's Museum of
Illusions and The Willesden Herald blog.

ISBN 9798729838813

Stephen Moran

Day of the Flying Leaves

Selected Poems

Willesden Herald Books

For Tessie and Craig

Contents

The Hunter-Gatherer Children of Dublin

The hunter-gatherer children of Dublin
Set out with jamjars or nets on bamboos,
Ranging far in the all-blossomed fields
Or with buckets out on a rocky shore.

The boys in school grey shorts and socks,
Pass unregarded by skipping girls,
Skipping, skipping, in gingham dresses,
Only wish - not. to. miss. a. loopio.

Close the lid and jar to catch
A redarse, footballer or shuggie
Busy bumbling pollen from clover
Always avoiding the unloved wasps.

Pinkeen shoals are nervous in ponds,
Frogspawn cowers amid green algae.
By the sea, in rockpools every crab
Sidles wary of toy plastic buckets.

Our tiring hunters return with exhibits
For a duly amazed but merciful adult,
Who says to set them free. While girls
Disregard, and pull up their ankle socks.

Eleven Homes

North King Street,
where a famous battle was fought in 1916
and where I bit the finger of a coochy-cooer.
I heard my first 78, "Who's Sorry Now?"
and tried to stack chairs to unlock a door.

Stephen Street Upper,
where I made my holy communion with Dublin
and we kids ran only as far as the corners.
Where now stands a department store,
the narrow stair & outside jacks no more.

Glasaree Road,
where the only car was a black Ford
Popular with running boards, Mr Talbot's,
and I memorised the reg J1235984,
and knew the boys and girls at every door.

Shangan Gardens,
with a staircase signed "Sam Nolan fecit"
and farm fields where the livelong days
we played football, talked and lazed,
and allocated somehow nubile mates.

Montpelier Rise,
a sojourn near Golders Green in a bedsit,
upstairs always redolent of Palmolive. It
was a family they wanted, which I did not,
so I flitted determinedly, leaving only a note.

Aylesford Street,
where some had division bells relayed.
Sous les toits, in a room we invaded,
an open gas meter the same one coin paid.
Westminster Hospital delivered our child.

Page Street,
also within the range of division bells
by mansion flats where bodyguards held
guns ready in jackets for Jim Prior to slide
into his limo by the bus stop alongside.

Churchill Gardens,
in a block named after Shelley with a view
over Chelsea Bridge across the river to
Battersea Park, where we'd walk and canoe,
take tea in the caf' and admire the pagoda.

First Avenue,
in a burnt-out house, renovated with council help.
Two up, two down, too small for four when
Nan came to stay and we of course cashed in
and leveraged luck into the bourgeois realm.

Peter Avenue,
The Case is Altered, Spotted Dog, Rising Sun,
crossroads for changing waves of immigrants,
Jewish, Irish, Australian, East European,
place of drudgery, striving, wassailing.

Cavendish Avenue,
in an enclave of roads between train tracks
where Piccadilly and Chiltern lines intersect
on the corner of Ealing, Brent and Harrow,
the child middle-aged, O.A.Ps, counting sparrows.

Visiting Molly

In memory of Molly Moran née Roche

It was always "Take it easy"
on schooldays, "have a day off."

In later life, "Why spend all your time
staring at that box? Go out and live."

Her Dublin maisonette had been immaculate,
daily pills laid out in a special box,

never a thing out of place, but
the electric kettle got burned on the hob.

Tipsy the terrier took her for walks
amid people known but names forgotten.

"Oh, I know some of them here are doolally."
Had I seen any open doors?

The plaster ornament dog in the courtyard
"would nearly...talk to you."

All I can do is change the subject when
she asks if I will take her home with me.

Now she arranges tissue papers on a tray
like ornaments on the old mantelpiece.

Says in the chapel here the priest asked,
"Now for our closing hymn, Molly,

will you sing O Mary This London for us?"
"Indeed I will." And she did.

As I was leaving, she walked halfway,
linking my arm, cheerfully.

The last words she ever said to me,
"I know you. I love you."

Morning Thoughts

Summer doesn't come around again
Because no two summers are the same.
If you're waiting for love to revisit
The parks and sofas and cars,
They're gone - under concrete,
Crushed and melted down, landfill.

No, summer won't come round again,
Look forward to the unborn,
Look backward to the long gone.
In winter, don't wish your life away.
There will be another season
For you, there will be a new day.

*

The mile-high club is grounded.
Sand dunes on that beach are in tier four.
There are cobwebs in the public toilets.
(Mind you, there always were.)
The back row of the flicks is nixed.
Wake up little Susy, it's over, we're dead.

*

You can look at it one of two ways.
You can say there's sodden paper
On the ground

Or

Sunlight shines on one side
Of the weed-grown back lane
Behind the shopping parade.

A smell of paint thinner is in the breeze
And the corner of an outdated poster
On a gable billboard
Opens like a door.

Day of the Flying Leaves

Our supple living green has turned to paper.
Rusty, soon-to-be shadows wander around.
The rushing south-westerly is a friend,
says anyway it's time to blow this town.

Autumn Rain

Autumn rain darkens terracotta tiles
to match the rotting leaves, tones down
white eaves, redbrick walls and gables,
soaking pavements from beige to brown.

Even the clouds, leading my way
at dusk, back down this road in Harrow,
kiss goodbye to pearlescent yesterdays,
thinking, echoing only woodsmoke.

I Wish I Could Wash My Brain

I wish I could wash my brain
with a hose, clean my mind out.

Maybe with a dishmop
I could expunge the longings.
Perhaps I could use a brush
to dislodge prejudices,
take a scouring pad to redundant memories.

Can you help?
Bash my mind on rocks in a nearby stream.
Don't stop till it's limp and pellucid.
Hang it out on a string line
with the dog's rug or other filthy things.

Put on your rubber gloves,
this is dirty work.

Walking in the Street with no Deadline

Walking in the street with no deadline
Is like taking a nap in the daytime
Fully clothed. Money in your pocket,
Sun beaming through. It's the world
Buzzing, not your ears. Find a seat,
A sunlit bench outside the library
Maybe, closed on a Sunday, nothing
To do, nowhere to go, no hurry to be
Home or visiting, just oneself, alone
Taking the long way home.

In Wormwood Scrubs Car Park

There's no such thing as waiting (W. Herald)

Spare a thought for inmates,
inpatients & chauffeurs,
eunuchs in harems,
call-handlers and gofers.
The wilderness waits at noon,
the firmament by night
but our lives are eked out
under fluorescent light.

The People Who Did Good Things

The people who did good things
and the people who did bad
are equally dead. Jesus and Hitler,
Mam and Dad, all sleep together
in the same big bed.

Atom splitters and dealers of dope
will light no more bombs
and blow no more smoke.
Monica from next door and Mohangi
the axe murderer, snooze like babies
and will wake no furtherer.

Humble grower of rice and joiner of racks
are stretched without the weight
of the sky on their backs. Kindly nurses
and torturers have all gone bye-byes
and are not coming back. Their feet
are no longer killing them.

Life is a Holiday from Non-Existence

There's lots to see and do,
And when it's time to go,
you wish you could stay
another week. But oh
in the end, you may say
we're tired and, after all,
we'll need another holiday
when we get home.

Unguarded Moments

If you walk without thinking how you're walking,
    that's the way you walk.
If you think without thinking where you're going,
    that's the way you think.
If you talk without thinking what you're saying,
    that's the way you talk.

Say my name.

Penny Arcade

And then there may be a moment
When you look into the eyes of the other
And realise they have always known.
She or he is ahead of you. They always
Cared. Or never cared at all.

Like those old mechanical horserace games.
In one race, she's ahead of you,
Everyone's ahead of you.
Yet in another game, you're far ahead
And can't be caught.

Who's Afraid of the Cold East Wind?

Herb Robert trembles,
not because the wind is strong
but because it's crazy.

Dandelion has wet himself
but won't let it get him down,
he's been through worse.

Rosemary doesn't know where to look,
it's all a bit of a mystery,
why do they bother?

Violet doesn't know why.
Poppy says don't be afraid.
Veronica says you should.

April shivers, a beast
has walked over her grave,
she hides in the chestnut tree.

Primrose lies low.
She sighs, she hopes
that May may come, come May.

Treen

The great trees, tall-masted,
heave away and sail by,
while I, who cannot move,
reach out and sway to them,
as they follow their green way.
For now it's Summer.

End of Winter

It's cold, it's wet, it's one of those days.
Yes, those days. Gifts of light,
Water, thoughts and air.

It's noisy and crowded on the train,
In the rush hour, but it's an hour
And it holds together one of our days.

In a moment of anguish, breathe
With your mind. It's a moment and
If it weren't there, you'd be dead.

We've had our days, our moments,
And come back for more.

All the Happy Moments

All the happy moments have whirled and twirled
and flown south for the winter. This morning
a few crazy stragglers defy the rain, and down here
the heavy minutes, shaking out their feathers.

Prelude and Fugue

Things aren't out to get you, it's you who are clumsy.
  The train wasn't late, you missed it.
It's not that what you wanted wasn't there, but you,
  you looked like you were moving, yet no more
than the swaying of trees that answer only to the wind,
  and move only to stay where they are.
Your actions are like the flickering of a candle flame
  as the time it measures dwindles
     to no more.

But trees don't walk. Don't wait for trees to walk,
  Go and caress them, whisper to their silence.
And if you quench a candle with your hand tonight,
  Relight it tomorrow night
     with your lips.

Reheating Tea

My forehead is a touch screen.
I take the edge and thumb-swipe time
forward, while regrets blur into pain.
One swipe and thirty seconds die
not with a bang but with a ping
on the microwave.

I have heard the burst of bombs
left by terrorist platelets,
sound travelling from the crater of a synapse
banging anvils onto hammers in my ear,
projecting dragons out through closed eyes,
and counted myself lucky
afterwards.

In spring an old man's fancy
likely turns to thoughts of wonder.
I open the blinds to let sunlight
blind me and send its flying vitamins
to anaesthetise lesions, and waken
hibernating hope cells with a splash
like witch hazel.

Shell is too strong a word
for this bubble, reflecting day's glare.
When you've floated around the sun
a few times, landed somewhere -
called it home and held in
the breath you were given. I wish
I had a shell.

Winter Thoughts

They put me in school. They do it to us all
and they teach us the alphabet and how to read,
how to add up and take away and memorise
the dates of battles, the names of kings,

while round outside the classroom the sun
illuminates the unread leaves and stirs
the untaught robin to sing his rhapsody
for which there is no do-re-mi, no metronome.

And we learn like Pavlov's dogs; how to please,
to supply the formula, to recite the text
we copied from the board and in return we get
rosettes, prizes, kisses, presents, Easter eggs.

But when the teacher has retired and our mams
and dads have forgotten everything or died,
we're left to wander abroad with nothing
but ciphers, tokens, money from a vanished state.

And late, now very late, the sun breaks through
a bare giant tree to lonely winter benches
where, as this afternoon, I wonder who to ask
to teach me how to read the day, the light

on public footpath signposts and leafmeal,
to diagram the last of the afternoon sun
warming a railway bridge in a country lane,
to derive the angles in a fine terrace below.

And I think of Yeats, Spender, Goldsmith,
walking through a classroom and being moved
to mystic reverie, fierce compassion, wonder.
But beyond the class there was a secret school

that taught us how to hear the ocean in a seashell,
to observe a crab blowing bubbles, the local names
for honeybees, how to draw houses, smoke & flowers.
Take me back to the school of streets and fields.

Reverie on a Theme

It's a hunger.
It's a raft in a flood.
It's a pitiful wound.
The tide in a lonely bay,
insanity of a saint,
the echo of silence,
sleepless weeping,
call of the nightjar,
triangulated moonbeam,
shared time,
when summer performs cartwheels.

It's a song on a loop,
merry-go-round of the heart,
plaintiff squeak of a mouse.
It's waiting for a letter,
the sound of your own name,
transfiguration of another's,
the grumble of a pet.

It's a mating call,
howl of the night wolf,
dove on a windowsill
waiting for bread,
help of a teacher for an idiot,
note left out on a table -

"Your dinner is in the oven."

The Possibility of Skipping

The time when seeing was believing has passed.
I thought window glass got in the way;
Open it – sash up, casement out –
And let me swim in that faith, unmediated.

Now there's a tealeaf in my right eye,
Or it looks that way but it's inside.
It's real and I've not been seeing spiders
After all, it's not *delirium tremens*.

And the woman in Specsavers sends me
From Kilburn to the Western Eye Hospital,
So I'm wading into the sea of faith
On the corner of Edgware Road.

Who turns here under the flyover,
Down where cars overhead can't see
And the flats are far back from the path?
Nobody, only me and Mary-Le-Bone.

I'm not seeing tealeaves, not reading
My future now. They come and go,
Swimming in that inner sea
Where dirty lenses never intervene.

Up ahead I notice a young woman
And just then she starts to skip along.
I think about dolphins at play,
Wonder if that's how they must feel.

I ask myself will I ever skip again?

I would like to lie and say I skipped
There and then in that concrete oasis
of St Marylebone, where I was alone.

Then the young woman turned left
Still skipping like a dolphin, on her way
To the flats far back from the path.
I thank her now and bless my eyes.

In the Waiting Room
of the Western Eye Hospital

I'm writing on my phone to while away
The crowded hours spent in this A and E.
A blur obscures my window, while the day
Unspools on Marylebone's evening street.
Here while taxis' amber lights go by,
A boy is screaming in the triage room.
The all-night clinic of the Western Eye
Hospital, where no one can see the gloom.
All are cheerful. Maisie, Mansoor, Abdul,
Concepta, Fatima. One or two have been
Here before and know the drill. They're full
Of London gallows humour often seen
When the worst comes to the best. But joy,
It's home for the fearful, now quiet boy.

Saturday Lie-In

Rattlegrating wheelets of the holiday bound,
monotonous cooing of pigeons in the eaves,
hill-gearing reveille of a diesel ghost bus.

Curtain run swish of the earliest ones,
hated clapping of the wake-up machine,
the rolling modality of bed locomotion,
and spreadeagle into diagonal torpor.

Return the postman to sender unread.
Not awake at this address for Witnesses,
Adventists, Latter Day Saints or salesmen.
Strip off, fall back, try to catch the last dream.

To Sunlight and on Walls

If you don't already know
why streets are like fresh-baked bread,
why old men play cards in the park,
on benches pulled together,
why a fallen tree waits for evening,

if you don't already know
the bandstand that enfolds a summer,
the cigarette that burns a journey,
silver rain that falls from the sun
to the ocean under a pier,

the heartbeat of concrete will never batter you,
the parchment of dried leaves will fall silent,
small birds will forget to sing,
and streams will not spring from stone.

Unless you pray to walls with light
and chant a hymn for morning traffic,
unless you shoulder up the clouds
and become the race of underground rivers,

you'll never see ascending to the sun
where no street was, a white wide street,
no row of houses will ever stand
transfigured into song,

and no train will bear you backwards drowsing
till you wake to some other voice,
other eyes, another
time, knowing
nothing.

To the People of New Earth

I think that I shall never see
Potato trees on G.581-c

We of the smaller planet,
Who make our dwellings from wood
And burn oil to drive our cars,
Send greetings to the people of New Earth.

If choosing a landing place in future
Please beware regions in dispute,
For your own safety, in case you're mistaken
For one of us, and shot.

We long to hear your poems of purple moon
And three-legged gazellaroos dancing
To the songcrows of midnight.

We crave Monster Munch that looks like us
And moon-dried tomatofig ice cream.

We're dying to know if your poets opine

Two girls in silk kimonos, both
Beautiful, one a Ferengi.

A special plea: don't diss the old culture.
Don't watch us on your "Vanishing World,"
Marching in our costumes into extinction.

Even if we believe in an impotent god,
Get sloshed on firewater and fight in the town,

We are not completely without worth.

Dear people of New Earth,
We have only just met, but
Please let's live in peace and,
If possible, bring us precious stones.

The Ghost of Sunday

Could've turned for home, but just went on
  the warmer way
and I met the ghost of Sunday on the corner
  of Bryan Avenue.
A memory of malt and hops
    and roasted coffee
must have blown in from St James's Gate,
  all the way.
It wasn't there, just the memory
    and Johnny Cash
and the sleeping city sidewalk,
  not O'Connell Street
just a few sunlit squares of concrete
    all to myself.

The Names of People who are Dead

The names of people who are dead
are like expired tokens, special offers
for something years ago,
used tickets from plays you saw,
went to see in theatres
that maybe now are bingo halls
or shopping malls,
the names of casts
in order of disappearance
and technicians too,
who privately could be impressed
to some extent, concerning the names
of people who are dead, or resting,
no longer players.

The Trajectory of Love

The trajectory of love is towards sorrow.
The trajectory of hate is towards shame.
We were born of the night to a bonfire of shadows.
Morning finds our bottle rockets
spent in other gardens,
where daylight falls on dew,
blackened ashes and dead grass.

For a Leaf

For a leaf whirled and drowned by rapids,
for a leaf pinioned under a beached hulk
or mouldering in a sodden hoof-print,
for all leaves,
through the Purgatory of decay
and the blessing of water,
returns the spring.
There is an afterleaf.

Proceedings of the Committee for Hopeless Love

Shall we take the previous minutes as read?
And the hours when morning brightened
To a day in the heart, out of mind, hot
With reckless words and shared heartbeats.

Our secretary sends his apologies, he's
Incapacitated by remorse and melancholia
After that joke that fell flat in the pub.
The first order of business is chemistry,

And Doctor Lizard has supplied the pills.
It's blue for warm and white for cool.
(Do let us know how you get on.)
Plans for the next event are already in hand.

And don't forget your longings and regrets,
Because you'll have the nights all to yourself.

Night Train

On an all-stations train to Wembley Park,
Inside's too bright, outside's too dark.
Mind the gap between train and platform.
Outside's too cold, inside's too warm.

Please don't obstruct or lean on the doors.
Some of us mumchance, others are bores.
The next station stop will be Waterloo.
Take all your personal longings with you.

Square

Dancing is an eco-friendly
way of burning emotions
in the form of joy.
Nuclear fusion occurs when
two people lean together.
There's a burst of heat
energy, and it's renewable.
Transform your misery
into happiness, and that
is alchemy indeed.

Crash

If crash investigators reach the scene of my life
it will immediately be apparent that my ailerons were
    fine.
Flapping, however, could not have saved me, for
if it could it surely would have. And equally nor
were my engines on fire, though I might have been
    bombed.
They may find my soul's black box, reassemble me
    in a hangar,
and put my life down, eventually, to human error.

Shaving Mirror

When I thought on getting old
It was never about days
Of full sun and icy breezes.
I thought about wrinkles,
A small world in my shaving mirror.
But I used to say to myself
All this misery is just euphoria
In the bank, I remember now.
And it was.

The Day Before Moving House

I gave the wild plants in my garden their last drink.
Goodbye strawberries. Goodbye hawthorn.
Goodbye to lilacs and little Lord Lambourne.
You've done me proud with fruit this year.
Goodbye plum tree and brambles at the end
Where Towser used to try, try to fetch the ball.
I give you, laurels, your last drink, and grass
Have water too, and drive the new ones mad.
Goodbye slow-growing Cypress Lawsonii,
I don't know what will become of you.
And littlest shrub with the aniseed sprays,
Your end will likely come this fall.
Have your last drinks, here's to you all.

The Goodbye Bird

Little white bird, little white bird, who are you?
I've been here twenty years and now I'm leaving,
You have never come before or do I know you?
There are so many souls for which I'm grieving.

Little white bird, little white bird, are you hiding?
I'll write my forwarding address on a may leaf.
And when autumn takes the leaf I'll be abiding
Somewhere else, somewhere else, beyond belief.

Canal of Days

Life is a canal, on which we are narrow boats
   with no reverse gear.
Each night, each sleep, is a lock.
We enter the lock and the water of yesterday
   is released,
till we emerge into tomorrow, to another gated
   day.
Behind us and above that again,
lie the days gone by. Ahead only today,
its prospect, its gate, its fall.
Gone the hundreds, hail the one.

Oh lucky swans!

Seasons

Don't look harshly on
the cold season that comes,
embrace it like an old friend
you might never see again.

Say something to Spring,
it's not without fears,
it's destined for the tragedy
of completeness.

Summer wants you,
Summer is not shy.
Summer won't bite you,
at least say Hi.

Take Autumn to the theatre,
something serious. Read
free verse from before the war.
But hurry.

In the Garden Today

Everything is better out of doors: drama, food,
music, love.

You can hear the wind in the trees,
the smallness of voices in the distance,
the similarity of gulls and schoolchildren's cries,
desultory clink of hammer on tin far away,
pecking of a neighbour's shovel on stone, angry jets.

The sheen of green-bellied flies does not go
unnoticed,
the visits and revisits of a rufous butterfly,
and some pigeon's one bar blues.

A hot day when the wind rushes through and cools
your ankles,
a dry day when the trickle of water nearby is a joy
to hear.
Sirens do not distract the terrier from chewing a stick,
working on it implacably, less concerned with
"noises off"
than with a hover-fly that dares to interrupt.

Leaves lit through by the evening sun
on top of a laurel mostly in shade,
bring a memory from a long-lost summer,
of a grand avenue with four rows of trees,
and side roads with small terraced houses below.

The End of Summer

"It's ours" - Bukowski

A breezy afternoon, the sun is partly overhead
on its journey from the street outside to
                         the back gardens.
The trees still hold their shadows below,
rustling with all their leaves.

Fruit is strewn everywhere, from street trees
and garden trees that overhang fences:
red apples, plums, cherries. There are more
black elder and orange firethorn berries
than the wood pigeons can eat.
Guano falls purple on a car windscreen.

The west facing high walls are at their brightest,
dazzling white and creamy pastel. The warbling
of conversations, words indistinguishable,
with folk rhythms and jags of mirth. Something
that sounds like a basketball bouncing
always when you listen, but never seen.

Traffic whines far off. The high wild pear tree
shivers like tambourines jostled by the breeze,
its sway and reach more passionate
                        and appealing
          than a dance.

Some small engine drones in a garden
                              on the next street.
                  The sky is ice-blue.
Telegraph wires shimmy a little, bounced
                                    by the breeze.
            All the talk in them weighs
                  nothing.

Unquiet Flows the Tolka

Bridge of Tolka, Drumcondra Park,
    spelter baluster, pewter spate.
Spectre of Swan's liturgy,
    philtre of Stac's refrain,
and peroxide Ida, acid exchange student,
your college green a prairie to our Botanics.
You sexed me with a buttercup, highly,
and yogi-sat akimbo. Oh Ida,
we shoulda. I'da.

Where are you now, bankrupt in Ohio,
    divorced in Union City?
Do men put their words into your mouth
    in Idaho?
Are you a mother of succour or did you die
    purple-hearted
by the tracks in Maine?

I'll seek you high and low in Isle au Haut,
I'll trade Manhattan for rosary beads
    and pray for an apparition,
I'll drop into every dive from Atlantic City
    to shining Zee,
and go over Niagara in a glass-bottomed boat,
looking for my Tolka naiad.

But should all peroxide Idas look the same,
I'll find out what Martinis are and drink them
    dry,
I'll down firewater without reservation
    in the Indian nations,

I'll find a night door and wait for you
        there as longing, unquiet
as the Tolka flows.

Towards an Index of Dad

In memory of Christy Moran

At the Fingal House by default on any free night
Brought home sweets every payday
Could sing like Giuseppe Di Stefano
Drove his new company car home all the way
                                    in first gear
Enjoyed Ken Dodd and Frank Sinatra
Found pretension insufferable
Gave his life to his work
Held his emotions in
Improvised words like "gobdaw" and "mixy-muxy"
Joked but laughed so much could hardly reach
                                    the punchline
Karl Marx was someone he had read
Liked the fat as well as the meat
Managed a clothing factory in the prime of his life
Never raised a hand to us
Owed allegiance to Manchester United
Played Young Covey in The Plough and the Stars
Questioned so-called intellectuals (perhaps as a result?)
Resided in working class Dublin all his life
Saved a little money for his funeral
Took me to join a boxing club, but we couldn't find it
Upheld standards but didn't preach
Ventured only as far as Old Trafford
Was loved by people I didn't even know,
                                    who cried in church

Annie

In memory of Annie Moran née Carey

Time out of mind Annie waited for us
before letting hunger
spirit her away.
"It was awful," they said.
"She was like one of those famine people,
you know, the ones you see on TV."

Could I have done more
for the dandling on her knee,
and the sing-songs,
and the butter dipped in sugar,
and cordial in the snug
with the flavour of Heaven?

I was growing a beard
when I visited last.
She turned away.
"That's not my Stephen," she said.
"My Stephen is a much nicer,
good-looking little boy."

Her feet never touched the floor
when she sat on the edge of her bed,
her grey hair straight-cut.
While mother made her up,
Annie worried about the locker thieves.
"They'd take the eye out of your head."

"When can I go home?" she asked.
"I want to go home."

But once when they tried,
she was afraid of all the traffic
and couldn't cope with money in the shops.

Her sons visited for years, then stopped.
Her sister never missed a Sunday.
My mother stepped in now and again,
and she never blamed my father.
"It got too hard for him to bear,
seeing her like that, for so many years."

Grandad's voice
was never heard in there
till the day of her obsequies
when he thundered basso profundo
to the usher,
"I am the husband."

As our black limo followed the hearse
through the gates of St Brendan's,
I said, "She finally got out of that place."

Valentine

He's buried there in Whitefriar Street
and they are buried too,
the disappeared,
all the types of you I fell for.

There are different tears
from different wellsprings,
ones that only know themselves
why they flow

silent as Marian statues
where the sackcloth urchins
behold miracles in blue and white,
silent as the widower
who dips fingertips only in a font
and waits
by the Stations of the Cross.

I drink holy water
from the tin cup on a string
and try to re-hydrate
the ashes and dust
of all those harbour girls.

Sleep, and let me sleep with you,
with St Valentine in Whitefriar Street.

Winter Solstice, Cardington Park

Overhead is opal turning sapphire,
Down to turquoise, and then blue.
The sun is cold upon the trees
On the far side of the reservoir.
A weeping willow, a reedy bank,
A few leaves, downcast, waiting.
And now three swans approach,
Looking for bread, expecting none.
They glance, reflect and dazzle
Like tomb light on the darkest day.

Breda Rainey

Breda Rainey you would
hammock in the rainy box
chaps sodden from the night dew.

Breda Rainey you wear
tiny leaves of the hedgerow
in your hair.

Breda Rainey you are,
though you heave a pushchair,
forever garlanded in box.

Again

Tell me a story
busy as sleeping,
older than childhood,
stranger than home.

Oh tell me a story
never before known,
the one I remember,
the one you forget.

And I will laugh for you
and close these eyes for you
and kiss you goodnight.

Again.

The Dolls' Hospital

There's a dolls' hospital in Dublin
Where shellshocked Actionmen rest
And dollies wait for limb transpops.
It's where ragdolls come to get stitches
And bears undergo kiddie dialysis.
Barbie is believed to have botox
Privately in the Outpatients Day Centre,
But Ken won't say. His lips are sealed.
Sindy is terminal in the hospice
Watching Sunset Boulevard on a loop.
There's a bench with a plaque dedicated
To the great Robinson Golliwog (
Killed by the cruel marmalade trade)
Where tin soldiers wear their rusty legs
And music box ballerinas lean
Forever akimbo, forever hopeful.
They'll soon be returning to their careers.

To a Young Woman

Never trust any man's love;
He is out to trample and leave you.
The flattery that turns your head
Is an insult wrapped up in a lie.

A flatterer is a deceiver
Who slanders you to his friends
And chases another woman
As soon as you turn your back.

Look for one who asks nothing
And gives all without a second thought,
One who will not tell your sins
Or belittle your wounded soul.

Within that person's eyes
You will find there in your mirror
The only one who knows
Just how beautiful you are.

To Myself, Aged Ten

Would you hear me if I could go back
And be a ghost from the future?
Could I tousle your hair,
Enfold you with arms of air?

Did I already, was it me
Making the champion marble win,
And turning coals into volcanoes
To entertain your lonely days?

Yes, yes! I was already there,
Making raindrops bounce for you,
Ensuring bumble bees were waiting
On every other patch of clover.

I never told you, you couldn't hear,
But I did everything by magic for you.

Sonnet for Dandy

Why should Dandy's obituary not be written
In as serious a manner as for Lord or Lady?
On Staverton Road each noontime he was sittin'
On the grass in front where it was nice and shady.

In the evenings he took his master walking,
A genial man who shouted greetings freely
across the street when he and I were talking,
But Dandy wasn't trusting strangers really.

Black, white and stocky, Dandy had a dour way.
I always said, "He'll bark at mine in a minute!"
And, after, he'd bark me and my dog on our way,
But truly, I don't think Dandy's heart was in it.

Tonight, I saw his master with a sleek new guide.
My question met a tearful answer, "Dandy? He died."

A Willesden Walk

The vast stainless steel plant
of the Capital City Academy
lies under mostly grey at first,

till turning east onto Donnington Road,
all of the sky, over half the world,
appears electric-lit or petrol blue.

North-northeast later,
under ice blue floes,
down to the cold of whitened ash.

And where would I be without
the ivory lightbox of an upstairs bay,
harmonising with a white
street light outside?

A war party of black cloud has halted
on the ridge of Dollis Hill.

At the corner back, a sort of prayer:
Vouchsafe me a view
of the sanguine amber, oh yes,
the peach red line, yes,
scrabbed in the west.

Taxidermy of The Spotted Dog

Clean gone are the sticky floors of centuries,
The fist-dented panels are stone dead and buried.
Its ceilings have swallowed their last tale of smoke.
Only the facade remains, tied up outside.

Bag Lady

For J*

Without a bag lady the earth would career
Out of its orbit and into the sun
She balances boxes of air and fear -
Nobody does it and it has to be done.

Without a bag lady cars would careen,
Forever speeding where children run.
She crosses, recrosses, slow and serene -
Nobody does it and it has to be done.

Without a bag lady inspecting the bins
Streetwalkers would walk the night alone.
She makes her own way, forgiving all sins -
Nobody does it and it has to be done.

** J. is a quiet soul who wanders the streets of Willesden
carrying several bags full of other bags and empty packets and
pulls a shopping trolley with more of the same. She is neither a
small lady nor very tall and she wears a bandanna.*

Cardboard City

In the darkness in the night
On the doorstep shivering,
When the moon sails left to right
Simon's soup is on the wing.

That fat lady with the urns
Comes from Kilburn to the Strand
With rosary beads and currant buns
And rabbit fit to beat the band.

Coppers twitch their mobile mics,
Suffer us to come to them.
Would you swap with Jesus Christ
On Calvary or Bethlehem?

Willesden Sunset, January

The lights come on and it's still not dark.
Shop windows light-up their mannequins.
Saw-toothed roofs of black terraces
are silhouetted in front of a fading sky.
Around the back of the high street
a few pale yellow window rectangles
take their colour from nearby lamps.
Another one or two are cold pastel blue
as though they were cut out of the sky.
The bright cold day sets on the horizon,
its hemline muddied to fag-ash grey.
In the supermarket car park drivers wait
while headlights swing by, silently.

Lines Between Day and Night

I am walking in the infralittoral zone
between day and night, between winter and summer.
The northern horizon is not sure it's still blue
as a bloody brown tide of cloud advances.
All the young trees are like kelp in a flood
trying to escape the rushing south wind.
More leaves than branch, unready for summer,
They're panicking over their drowned blossoms.
A patchwork of flagstones, no two alike,
kaleidoscopes greys with beiges and white.
Soon every colour will submit to shadow.
Green places will have hollows instilled.
Daisies and dandelions will close their eyes,
and streetlights will stand sentry till dawn.

Inisheer - 1975

Above the half door, a beach;
above that again, the sea.
The morning ferry from Galway
anchors in the doorway
and waits offshore in the sun.

Aran sweaters are navy blue
and such, not many white.
The ferrymen, hard as the sea,
are readying their currachs,
which are also fishing boats.

This island has no police,
no cars, no roads, no harbour.
The people speak Irish
and the tiny stonewalled fields
have rabbits and a donkey or two.

This side faces the mainland.
There's a pub. That's it.
They close when you finish drinking.
We never knew and kept them awake,
then staggered out under the stars.

One of them was zig-zagging.
Who knew we couldn't fix it,
on the rocky path we walked,
stopping, sitting, starting again,
mystified and drunk with life.

I was remembering Howth head

when three of us lay in the dark
in an all-enveloping blackness,
with constellations above
and a boat light crossing the bay.

That sober night you said
"Who can look on this
and fail to find wisdom?"
I recall it was your wisdom
that always saw us through.

A little sandy beach,
sheltered by rocks,
we sunbathed but never swam.
The cove was full of jellyfish
blown in by last night's gale.

I ate something like wild garlic
stupidly, luckily not poisoned.
Walking where skuas swooped
to threaten our heads, we found
a ruin half-buried in the sand.

It was a church from the age
of saints and scholars, hungry,
not tall or else they stooped
to pass under the low lintel
into their pious stone hall.

Our blasé plaster living rooms
might be bigger now than this
place where monks huddled
and chanted in Latin, fearful,
euphoric and awestruck.

Another mile to the final cliffs
where sheered walls of tawny rock
face the edge of the world.
Did they venture in twos, singly,
or all together to this western shore?

They prayed to God of the Atlantic
for their feeble, perilous lives.
They prayed for the flat world, finite
under a dome of sky, waiting
for the terrible Judgment Day.

Next stop America, we know now.
But for them the ineluctable fury
of the Atlantic was proof
that they were small, very small,
and so are we, the same.

The wavelets turn rollercoaster
only halfway to the ferry, leaving.
It's too late then to set the price
when they ask. Whatever it is,
we have to pay the currach men.

Falling Asleep

Walk to the window,
part the sepia curtains,
peep out,
see the albino street.

Heavy and weak,
turn into bed.
The small of your back
Is a hollow box-kite.

Can you breathe
if you fall asleep prostrate?
Is there comfort
halfway between side and back?

Replay the words
everyone said today.
Too late,
you know the answers now.

Grotesque faces
made of coal and shadow
glint in the blindness.
If only you could paint them.

A falling start
and now your carefree spirit
floats over
the echoing, empty playground.

Canary Dream #4

canary
in a sun-room
when I
try to put it
in a cage
 it turns
      into
    flakes
of
   pure yellow
        that
        scatter

 in the air

   and out the window

Wake Up Call

Leeds sleeps rough.
The night does not descend
but rather abandons her
to the horizon.

She has made her bed
out of unmade car parks
that pit and flood
and reflect the void.

The station hotel
is the foyer of Hell
where uniformed demons
guard the forecourt.

Inside this cruise ship
all walk in a swell,
leave shoes outside doors
and settle down to porn.

Blue Nun from the mini-bar
is followed by Pils.
The free preview is enough,
it won't show on the bill.

You are dried-up and sleep
the burnt sleep of the damned.
Trains shunt and hammer you awake
From nightmare with a yowl.

In the morning you will go

where the natives swarm,
be a stranger in their offices
and eat curd tarts for lunch.

You'll pass by the night club
where Leeds footballers sank
too many drinks and kicked
two Asian boys nearly to death.

The suits are astir now,
squirming with their itchy groins.
Stilletto P.A.s are powdered, ready
to gun their Beemers round the square.

The high Victorian statuary
is bigger than all these boutiques,
travel agents and burger bars
crushed into one paper cup.

It's Easier to Tangle than to Untangle

Seconds and moments don't follow, they
permute.
One on the microwave countdown cannot
be understood as two together tangle
with the next and prior but those are only
yours. That dusty vase on a shelf has its own
infinity. The spider on the floor, a few more.

Refugees

We are young, our whole lives ahead of us,
When we take a chance on a rusty hulk.
Terrified at last to be locked below deck,
Never wanted so many to push on board.

The Mediterranean is calm, so they say, but
With bodies crushed together, no provisions
And no facilities, death is never far away.
All long for Lampedusa, tolerance, a new life.

It is night now and a patrol is sighted,
A hubbub arises and the old tub lists.
Before you can think about home, here or there,
The sea is upon us all, this is our tomb.

In villages and towns, the old are bereft,
Some wives too and youngsters. Will they ever
Hear, or will they be left to surmise,
When no call from Europe ever comes?

(2016)

I Wonder How My Body Will Burn

I wonder how my body will burn?
It's cruel to burn my toes, so
ill-used and loyal, monstrous
to roast my thighs and shins,
strong bones reduced to ash.
Good riddance to the private
parts, fat lot of good they did
me. Stomach, what a terrible
waist. Halfway. Oh, here we go.

I Still Wear Shirts

I still wear shirts I used to like
when I used to like shirts,
going to places I used to go
when I liked going to places.

For old times' sake I'll pull on
the same old thing I used to pull on
when I was fond of pulling on
that same thing I pull on now.

Oh but it's not the same.

Daffodils are Ugly / Apology

Daffodils are ugly, egomaniacs
blowing their own trumpets,
playing silly buglers, monotonous
"Does my bulb look big in this" bimbos.
Oh but we love them, we love them senseless
because we know they're better than us.

Apology

For avoidance of all doubt,
daffodils are lovely, hapless
horse-like, handsome flowers.
I apologise to daffodils,
they cannot help themselves,
it's the way they are brought up.

Through the Open French Doors

Through the open French doors,
between the woods and the lane,
a stave of power lines
with birds for notes.

I lift the lid on the piano
and start to play them.

"She is far from the land"

Mismatch

If your cups don't chase each other round the cup tree,
I will arrange them so they do.
But you may not be the one for me,
And I may not be the one for you.

Chirrup

The free birds are giving up their singing,
The first thing they do each morning is login.
Ostriches have learned to wear bras
And bolster their self-esteem with mindfulness.
Meanwhile rabbits are mesmerised by television;
They can't take their eyes off 24-hour news.
Even slugs are slowly moving with the times,
They all speak pure Estuary with glottal stops.
In hives there is a new type of bee, it seems,
Not a worker, a drone or a queen but a flaneur.
The flaneur bee is too heavy to fly and couldn't care
Less.

The Road Not Taken

On seeing two signposts pointing opposite ways to
Edenderry, one that said 8 miles and one that said 10

She bid me take her hither,
I bid her take me yon
But I being young would dither
And now she's taking John.

Down by Edenderry
Our rendezvous was set
But I went by the long road
And now she's with that get.

So listen all you geezers
On Erin's craggy coast
Always take the short cut
Or else your arse is toast.

Nearly Man

Ah me and Carmel Kavanagh from Navan
In a caravan in Cavan
Almost consummated our mirage.
Then a one night couldn't stand
With Anna from Knockananna
In Banna sur la Plage.
I nearly humped Dymphna from Crumlin though,
On a drumlin near Drumshanbo
But never knowingly akimbo,
She dumped me at Crimbo,
Which ruined my image
In Kimmage.

Tommy Maher's Irish Bar

Welcome in, have a skinful
Gunga Din, it's not sinful.
Take a drink and only think
That Jesus Christ's own advice
Was get more in, partying
With James & John, dusk till dawn
At Tommy Maher's Irish bar.

Tread Softly, for you Tread
on Murmurons from Jupiter

Don't dig it up, don't tramp it down,
The wildflower purple crown vetch,
It's that they eat and that alone,
Potatomen from the planet Kvetch.

Many extra-terrestrials here
Are tiny and struggle to survive.
Bamlards from Gliese five-eighty-four
Subsist entirely on baby chives.

Extraterrestrials like the Balleyes
From Venus can hardly be seen,
They're so tiny, and so specialised,
They live on the fumes from Windowlene.

Ode to a Bedsock

The life of a bedsock is not very onerous.
It does the opposite whatever its owner does.
When you hit the hay its work must begin,
Together, usually, with its identical twin.
Bedsocks are harmless. Their idea of play
Is to wander about on a mattress all day.
So mind the Geneva Convention, fellows,
And never confine them under the pillows.

Outtakes from Spoon River Anthology

*

Tinnitus Young

Martha Postlethwaite hunted me for 20 years
Till at last I lay panting under her flashing teeth.
She stole her prize but in the taking
My heart burst and she lived forty years a widow.
Na na na na na.

*

Trod Strongly

As a child I liked nothing better
Than to roll and tumble in the hay in Art Poorly's barn
But on my first day as a hand on the harvest
I daydreamed and got rolled and tumbled
By Art's new combine harvester
And so I met my baleful end.

*

Mildred Fulbright

The local party chose me to present our town's gift
When Taft's whistlestop train arrived.
I waved as the President left and he waved back.
Joe Fulbright was the proudest stationmaster in our
        state.
But when Washington shut the railroad down
Pa took to drink and overturned our wagon

Into the Spoon River one icy night.
He tried to save me but my hair caught in waterweed.
Now he's a Democrat.

*

Ulick Angstrom

They said it was a shame how I never ventured into
        town
Though I had travelled to the onion domes of the
        Kremlin
And to the minarets of Aya Sofia
And from the cafés of Paris
To the street barbeques of Manila.
But with all my knowledge
I brought home an embarrassing disease
Right when Doc Slein's daughter took over the practice
And that's what got me in the end.

*

Valerie de Valera

To this much at least they all could agree:
Discretion was not the best part of Valerie.

*

Pleat Muggins

Dory and Cory Muggins named their son Pleat
After an ancestor who sailed with Vasco Da Gama.
He was surly and never learned, though able,

And massacred his family at the age of 16.
When hanging judge Crudmore asked
If he had anything to say in mitigation,
All he said was, "My name is Pleat."

*

Mickey Pride

Here lies Mickey Pride.
He laughed till he cried.
He cried till he died.

*

Benjy Doone

"I shat myself, I pissed the bed,
I thought this & that, I lost my head,
I loved three or two or one.
That's the autobiography done."

At the Poetrycraft Store

A quarter pound of mixed metaphors -
Not too much, about a fistful will do.
And like a sandwich bag of similes,
A sack of anaphora, now lemme see,
A sack of anaphora, oh yes,
Just a small tin of irony (I never use it)
And some personification,
If you have it, Poesy.

He Wishes for the Green and Silver Bits

After WBY

Had I the heavens' embroidered circuitboards,
Enwrought with silver of solder and flux
The boolean half charge of decision scores,
Resistors and matrices of maybes and musts,
I'd encrypt there the tales of Arabia for you.
But I being poor have only my wee jests;
Tread softly because you tread on my jesticles.

Early Licence

There is a pub in Dublin town
They call the Morning Star,
And many a pint they pull at dawn
For dungareed cattlemen there,
Whose lowing beasts, corralled around
By iron railings in a queue,
Pine for their owners in the lounge,
Drinking, like big breeders do.

Oh One-by-Three

Oh one-by-three
  shamrock mystery
all-in-one
  with the father and son,
is mother the ghost there
  in a burqa of feather?

Holy
  ghost, father, son,
holy
  past, present, future,
holy
  shame, blame, fear

were you tempted really,
  did you really fall,
  why do you punish yourself?

Oh Flaking Gilt Money Box

Oh flaking gilt money box of St Francis,
    save us.
Oh electric candles of St Mary,
    pray for us.
Oh plaster saints whose names we know,
    blush for us.
Oh sanctuary light, oh holy lantern of Jesus,
    never go out,
        never doubt our existence.

St Paul Said It All

St Paul said it all
snail mail.

St Peter is not a tweeter
but St Mary is always online.

The father has no email,
no one can reach him
except through the son.

The spirit translates pages into any language
with comical results.

Outtake from The Da Vinci Code

My first is Balaam but not in ass
My second is in Noah but not in flood
My third is in Virgil but not Catullus
My fourth is in very but never in good
In my pelt through the desert I fly
Who the hairy hell am I?

Whitton Avenue

By the corner house there used to be
Shrubbery and a recumbent tree
Where small birds liked to play.
Now there's a block-paved yard,
A useless space for man or bird
But the landlord likes it that way.

Pain and the Hollywood Stars

Robert Mitchum's expression says, I have a little pain
       but it's nothing I can't handle.
Burt Lancaster says, I can bear it, I can bear it, how
       about you?
Gregory Peck seems to say, I fear I might be next but
       I'll be ready for the day.
Paul Newman of course has heard about it, would like
       to talk about it, if you wish.
Steve McQueen is dead, died of pain, always looked like
       he would.
Which brings us to Jimmy Dean and all those other
       martyrs, well they got what they wanted.
But Eastwood, now he offers pain, you want it, (well do
       you punk?), there's plenty to go round.
Bogart is not really thinking about his own pain, his
       terrible pain, he only wants to ask about yours.
Edward G: I've got it, now you're going to get it.
Cagney thinks it's all the same, joy or pain, best get it
       while it's going.
Brando: What have you got, I'm hedging my bets but
       I'm thinking how can I get out of this before it
       hurts.
James Mason: Don't talk to me about pain, my back is
       killing me.
George Sanders is thinking, pain you say - we'll see
       about that.
There were women too, they knew it served us right.

But that was all a long time ago.

There May Be Horrors

There may be horrors on the floor of the sea
and ever more sorrows down a stony road,
but we are not at the bottom of the sea
and where this road winds nobody knows.
So while there's still rosé from France
and seasick priests are going green,
might I have the honour of this dance
with you, my ginger Rosaleen?

The First Time the Earth Went Round by the Sun

The first time the Earth went round by the Sun
it was a rainy morning.
Rocks sat back nonplussed, as if to say
"What the hell just happened?"
and decided to take a nap,
time enough to unpack later.
But after dark awoke perhaps, jet-lagged.
A constellation that used to be there,
gone like an old bedroom
with the bed beside a different wall.

The second time the Earth went round by the Sun
must have been a Tuesday,
St Patrick's day, as it fell that year,
and it rained again.
Rock Tours had gone bust it seemed,
so we were there for the duration.
It was warm at first, then a bit too hot.
That's the trouble with these places.

Yadda, yadda.
Wednesday, oh for Pete's sake
it's bucketing down. Let's have a lie-in -.
Huh, something just crawled over my face.
Shut up, it's only a hare.

The, what was it, fourth day it never let up,
seriously large floods.
Overheard two nudists nattering,
Is it me or is it getting hotter?

Yes, that'll be because we're in the northern
        hemisphere.
Say again?
What the hell is that? Ugh!
Don't say ugh here my dear,
it only plays into their preconceptions.

The fifth day the Earth went round by the Sun,
we had to make our own fun,
playing poohsticks and washing in a rain-barrel.
Wouldn't it be great
if only it would stop raining? Then a miracle,
the clouds parted and fell quiet.
Only under the trees it was still raining
and for the first time there were hills,
blue black hills,
at the end of every road.

And on the Eighth Day

Refreshed after a day off on Sunday,
God went back to work.

On the eighth day he created poliomyelitis, smallpox,
bubonic plague, influenza, acne, narcolepsy
and Total Amelia syndrome.
He worked in a frenzy, the ideas poured out of him.

On the ninth day he created volcanoes, earthquakes,
        tsunamis,
 hurricanes, tornadoes, mudslides and droughts.
Again, he was inspired and elaborated his new
        inventions for hours.

On the tenth day he populated the firmament
with a sprinkling of asteroids, meteors and comets,
millions of them on random paths, and that
gave him the biggest laugh of all.
He felt that if he laughed while creating them,
others would too when they saw them coming.

On the tenth day he thought,
I'm becoming a bit too predictable,
let's dig a bit deeper and he invented depression,
narcissism, paranoia, and schizophrenia.
It will add weight to the whole scene -
sombre, off-beat, violet-coloured interludes.

On the eleventh day, he thought, "Follow that!"
And then he thought, "It's all a little too obvious.
The trick is to go from bad to worse,

to be cruel to your characters.
Let me think about it."

On the twelfth day, he spied on the people
and saw with dismay how they looked at each other
with love. That was not in the plan.
For a while he was stumped.

Then he woke up in the middle of the night of the
        thirteenth day
and he wrote it down on a post-it note.
"Death."

Crazy Paving

*On seeing a picture, not necessarily from Gaza, of an
armed soldier hiding in a doorway, with two children in the
street nearby (Unicef193-0634 / Betty Press)*

Crazy paving, crazy wall,
Concrete floors. When curfews fall
F-sixteens will come to call.
Rocket bye baby, the cradle will fall;
Down will come gunmen, mothers and all.

Iron shutters, iron gates.
Out of sight, a soldier waits
On girl and toddler, under eights.
The elder with her friend debates
Oblivious to their future fates.

Not the chosen, not the just,
They are children of the dust,
When hovels with no papers must
Be razed in order to adjust
Collateral in a stateside trust.

Mockingbird

Hush little baby, take your rest;
Papa's gonna buy you a suicide vest.

And if that suicide vest don't blow,
Papa's gonna make you a bomb to throw.

And if that bomb won't kill someone,
Papa's gonna get you a tommy gun.

And if that tommy gun goes wrong,
Papa's gonna build you an atom bomb.

And if that atom bomb won't blast,
Papa's gonna make you a plague to cast.

And if that plague turns back on us,
Papa's gonna buy you a house of dust.

And then before the sun goes down,
You'll look sweet on every wall in town.

The Weight of Words

The number of all the raindrops that have ever fallen on
        England
times all the snowflakes that ever fell on Japan
by the number of jelly beans in a very big jar,

that number of words,

would not outweigh a pinch of wild cotton
as would make a pillow
for a fairy.

Ballad

It is the hour of waking alone.
One jet is unzipping the sky.
Boxwood hedges await me
And watch my feet go by.

The pines are hiding their scent
With the privet for tonight.
They hold no interest this morning,
Enervated by so much light.

The dead grocer is still alive,
Surly, serving in the shop,
Henpecked in a biscuit coat
At the parade where buses stop.

Joan Gentle is near me now,
Worth marrying just for the name.
She often gets on the sixteen,
But she is dead just the same.

Two friends linking arms as always
On the path by the flower bed
Will never get to hear about TaTu,
Aids or crack, because they're dead.

The conductor with nothing to say
Still hears the sister squeal
"That's my brother, that's my brother!"
He too has passed under the wheel.

Maisie of the hot pants is a zombie
In the kiosk selling cigarettes
And I will buy ten Senior Service
And inhale without any regrets.

There's where Vicky lives over the shop.
She cuts hair and makes mothers blonde.
They still share tea and drink gossip
Even though they're beyond the beyond.

Their blueprints are filed under gone
Missing, and presumed unknown.
Although we are dead, we're alive -
All in the hour of waking alone.

Printed in Great Britain
by Amazon

62275513R00073